Welcome

Welcome to All Saints!

   This ancient parish church and its predecessors have shaped the life of Kingston for well over one thousand years. The first kings of England were crowned here, and the town with its markets and businesses grew up around the church.

   Since those early days All Saints has been the centre of the Kingston community, and it remains integral to the life of our town to this day. People have come here for meetings, celebrations and commemorations, and a wide variety of cultural events, while worship and prayer continue to underpin it all.

   At their best, churches meet people where they are and encourage them in a greater fullness of living. This has been the texture of All Saints' past and remains its goal for the present and the future.

   We hope you enjoy your visit to our church, soaking in its history and enjoying the promise that the building proclaims, and that your enjoyment will be enhanced by reading about its story, and the ways in which the life of our nation and town are entwined in it.

ished by All Saints Church, Kingston upon Thames, 2015
right © All Saints Church, Kingston upon Thames

t cover image
aints Church in 1798.
gston Museum and Heritage Service

Contents

One of two Daniel King engravings of All Saints Church, c. 1650. These are the earliest known images of the church.

t end of All Saints
e 1840s.

Introduction

The parish church of All Saints was built in the twelfth century at the heart of a royal estate in which a town would develop. Even before the church was constructed, this was the place 'Where England Began' – the place where Athelstan the first true King of England was crowned, and where Church and Crown formally agreed to support each other.

All Saints today continues to sit at the heart of Kingston, serving a growing congregation in a thriving London borough. The church has stood here for 900 years and is now a Grade I listed building, the only one in the town. All Saints continues to adapt to the needs of the community it serves as a place for meeting, celebration and culture, whilst remaining true to its foundation as a place of worship and prayer where all may find a moment's peace.

Today's church includes beautiful Victorian stained glass, intriguing memorials commemorating past lives, and even a stone fragment older than the church itself. The East Surrey Regiment Memorial Chapel sits in the north-east corner, to the east of our wonderful Frobenius organ. As you make your way around the church, explore how worship and the very fabric of the building have adapted over nine centuries, discover the building's secrets and learn more about the lives played out here. Through its architecture and memorials, the church reveals the fascinating history of the town and the nation.

Great west window.

Where England Began

Coinage of the Saxon kings.

18th century portrait of King Egbert.

Kingston has long been celebrated for its royal connections and significance as the birthplace of our nationhood and monarchy. From at least the early ninth century Kingston or 'Cyningestun' was a royal estate of the Saxon kings.

Kingston sat on an island site near the head of the tidal River Thames, on the border of the kingdoms of Wessex and Mercia, symbolic for kings who wished to unite Angles (north of the Thames) and Saxons (south of the river).

Kingston's royal connections are first evident in the record of King Egbert's Great Council in 838, which was held here. It is recorded as happening 'in that famous place called Cyningestun', the name denoting an established royal estate, probably including a consecrated building. At the Council, the king and Ceolnoth, Archbishop of Canterbury, formed an alliance, and Ceolnoth probably anointed Egbert's son Ethelwulf to be his successor.

It has been traditionally claimed that seven tenth-century Kings of England were crowned at Kingston: Edward the Elder (900), Athelstan (925), Edmund (940), Edred (946), Edwy (955), Edward the Martyr (975) and Ethelred (978). The Anglo-Saxon Chronicle records two, Athelstan and Ethelred, and Edred's coronation is confirmed by a charter. For the other four, the evidence is late or speculative, and it was only in the thirteenth century that all seven coronations were attributed to Kingston. The only tenth-century coronation to be recorded as being held elsewhere is that of Edgar (959-975) at Bath in 973, when he had already been king for fourteen years. Several historians now consider that this event was exceptional, and that Edgar would have been anointed and crowned soon after becoming king.

Where England Began

King Athelstan depicted on his own coinage.

The most notable of these Saxon kings was Athelstan, grandson of Alfred the Great. He was crowned here on 4th September 925 in a ceremony which laid the foundations for our modern coronation service, down to the coronation of Queen Elizabeth II in 1953. Athelstan first greeted his people in the marketplace before entering a church, which probably stood on or near the site of our church. Athelstan was the first King to be consecrated with a crown placed on his head, rather than a helmet. For the first time the coronation service laid out the responsibilities of the monarch and his people to each other, and the Christian hymn Te Deum was sung as it is now.

Athelstan went on to become the first true King of England, as it was during his reign that regional kingdoms were united as one nation. As King of the English from 927, he was the first English king to conquer northern Britain. Athelstan was a particularly successful soldier and defeated a combined army of Scots and Vikings at the battle of Brunanburh in 937.

Kingston's coronation stone is a block of sarsen sandstone which may have been recovered from the site of St Mary's chapel next to All Saints. By 1793 *The Ambulator* was reporting that it was the stone on which the Saxon kings sat while being crowned. This tradition, which culminated in the stone being mounted on a plinth and surrounded by railings in the market place in 1850, is now itself an important part of Kingston's history.

Portrait of the tenth century Saxon king Athelstan from a thirteenth century royal manuscript.

Portrait of King Athelstan, artist unknown, c. 1515. This portrait is one of two wooden panels forming part of a Saxon Kings frieze, discovered in 1813 by Alfred John Kempe at Baston House, Kent.

11

East Kingston Surry

All Saints and Kingston

Saxon cross shaft.

A consecrated building probably stood on the site at the time of Egbert's Great Council of 838, and there must have been a church or chapel, perhaps of wood, by the time of the tenth-century coronations. The fragment of a late tenth- or early eleventh-century cross displayed in the church may have come from the churchyard of a church of this period. St Mary's Chapel was built in the eleventh century, probably before or shortly after the Conquest of 1066, and there may also have been a church on the site of All Saints: the Anglo-Saxons often built two consecrated buildings in close proximity. There was a church at Kingston in 1086, when Domesday Book was compiled: the entry for Kingston includes the words 'ibi ecclesia' ('a church there'). The large size of the later parish, stretching from East Molesey to Kew, suggests that the early church in Kingston served as a minster (a large and important church) for this extensive area. Clergy at the minster would have taken responsibility for the religious needs of the whole parish until chapels were founded at Thames Ditton, East Molesey, Petersham and Sheen (which was later renamed Richmond).

Any earlier church on this site was probably destroyed prior to the construction of St Mary's in the latter half of the eleventh century. All Saints was built in the twelfth century. The church and its endowments were given to Merton priory, which appointed its vicar and was responsible for the repair of the chancel until the Reformation. It was also in the twelfth century that Kingston developed as a town, and a royal charter was granted in 1200. A market is first recorded in 1242 but almost certainly existed earlier. Farmers brought crops and animals from the surrounding area and Kingston was a natural resting place for travellers between London, Guildford and Portsmouth. The church was important in the development of the town, stimulating demand for local goods and services. Its bells marked the opening and closing of business and repairs and rebuilding gave work to local craftsmen and tradesmen. Thus developed a community characterised by partnership between town, trade and church.

All Saints Church History
The Early Centuries

Memorial in Holy Trinity Chapel, probably to Clement Mylam, 1496.

Kingston Lawyer and Surrey MP Robert Skerne and his wife Joanna.

All Saints Church, as originally built in the twelfth century, was cruciform with a tower at its centre. To the east of the tower was the chancel, and to north and south there were transepts probably of equal depth to the present aisles.

Nine centuries later, few remains of the original fabric can be seen. During nineteenth century restorations an original Norman west door was uncovered, but was judged incapable of being preserved and unfortunately destroyed. All that remain of the twelfth-century church in the present fabric are stones where the westernmost nave pillar in the south arcade meets the west wall. It is probable that these stones formed part of the wall of the Norman nave. These are shaped with an axe and not a chisel, an implement which came into use later. The core of the tower, now masked by later work, also dates from this time, and other features which were re-used by later builders are on display.

In the late thirteenth century the tower was rebuilt, and by about 1400 the nave had been rebuilt with wide aisles. Merton priory was ordered by bishop William of Wykeham to repair the chancel roof in the fourteenth century, and towards the end of the fifteenth century the chancel was enlarged to its present size.

Chantry chapels were founded and endowed by wealthy citizens who would employ a priest to say prayers for their family members and assist their souls' journey to heaven. St Mary's Chantry was founded on the south side of the church in 1459 by local man William Skerne for prayers for his family, including his uncle Robert Skerne and his wife Joanna, who are commemorated by a memorial brass still in the church.

Groups of less wealthy local people could also form groups to jointly endow a chantry chapel. For example, the Holy Trinity Chapel (now the East Surrey Regiment Memorial Chapel) was built on the north side of the chancel in 1477 by the Guild of the Holy Trinity. A thirteenth-century moulding on the west side of the arch from the chancel into this chapel suggests that it replaced an earlier chapel.

All Saints Church History
The Later Middle Ages

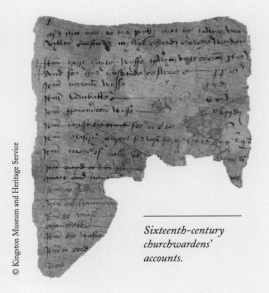

Sixteenth-century churchwardens' accounts.

As Kingston became larger and wealthier All Saints had been extended to accommodate larger congregations and provide more altars for the saying of Mass together with statues and pictures for private devotion. The wall painting of St Blaise, patron saint of woolcombers and people with throat diseases, who was also believed to be able to cure sick cattle, illustrates both the importance of the wool trade and the needs of local people.

A visitor would have been struck by the richness of the interior of the church with its bright colours and rich furnishings. It held an impressive number of altars and priests to serve them. The chancel, the preserve of the clergy, would have been divided from the nave, where the congregation gathered, by a rood screen showing Christ on the cross with the Virgin Mary and St John. Worship at this time involved considerable ceremony and visual display. The Mass was sung in Latin, which most of the congregation would not have understood, although they would have been aware of its significance as the sacrament of Christ's body and blood.

All Saints drew its congregation from a wide surrounding area and the expenses of the building and worship were borne by a compulsory church rate. The churchwardens were responsible for the maintenance of the fabric and their account book beginning in 1503 shows us the range of work required on the building and its contents. The churchwardens were also responsible for the Kingham May game and Robin Hood play, entertainments which toured Surrey towns and villages and raised money for the church.

*Painting of St Bl
dating from the
15th century.*

17

All Saints Church History
The Reformation and after

Memorial to Richard Mayo, died 1695.

Memorial to the ten children of Edmund Staunton.

During the Reformation, between the 1530s and 1560, the religious landscape of England underwent many changes. The first major change to affect Kingston, in 1538, was the dissolution of Merton priory, which had been the patron of the church, appointing its vicar and maintaining the chancel, for four hundred years. The language of public worship changed from Latin to English and the Books of Common Prayer of 1549 and 1552 introduced new forms of worship. Chantries were abolished in 1547 and in the reign of Edward VI (1547-53) inventories were compiled of church furnishings and vestments which were mostly confiscated. The changes in worship were reversed under Mary (1553-8), but the accession of her sister Elizabeth restored the Book of Common Prayer in slightly revised form in 1559 and removed most of the furnishings restored in the previous reign.

The new services of Morning and Evening Prayer (Matins and Evensong) became the main services, and preaching became more important than the celebration of the Mass, now called the Lord's Supper or Holy Communion.

During the religious turbulence of the sixteenth and seventeenth centuries All Saints would have lost much of its colour. Altars were dismantled and the rood screen was removed. Coloured glass, images, statues and wall paintings were removed. Although the Church underwent a limited programme of beautification in the 1620s, All Saints' interior remained comparatively sombre.

Some parishioners considered that the reformed Church of England had retained too much of its Roman Catholic past. From the 1580s onwards, Kingston was a centre of those people known as Puritans, who wished to move the Church of England's practice and organisation in a more radical Protestant direction. John Udall delivered sermons in Kingston which challenged the Elizabethan Settlement, and in some of his publications Udall went so far in attacking the Queen that he was in danger of being executed for high treason. In 1633 a noted Puritan, Edmund Staunton, became vicar. A zealous preacher, he was a Parliamentarian during the Civil War. He became a member of the Westminster Assembly, which replaced the Book of Common Prayer by a 'Directory of Worship' and instituted a system of church government without bishops. Staunton is remembered in the church by a memorial to his ten children who all died while he was vicar.

Edmund Staunton served as mentor to Richard Mayo, minister of All Saints from 1658 to 1662. Mayo, like Staunton, was a Presbyterian, and following the Restoration of Charles II in 1660 he was 'ejected' from the church in 1662 because of his opposition to the return of the traditional government and worship of the Church of England. He was followed by a number of parishioners, the start of a congregation which was to be the ancestor of the present-day Kingston United Reformed Church.

In 1703 the church spire topped with a weathercock, which was the pride of local townspeople, was destroyed in a storm. The tower was so badly damaged it had to be dismantled; it was rebuilt in brick in 1708, but the spire was not replaced. In the 1720s the aisles were rebuilt in brick and given plaster ceilings, joined by fashionable classical style pedimented doorways at the west end and at the entrances to the north and south transepts. In the seventeenth and eighteenth centuries high box pews and galleries were introduced to provide more seating for the growing local population.

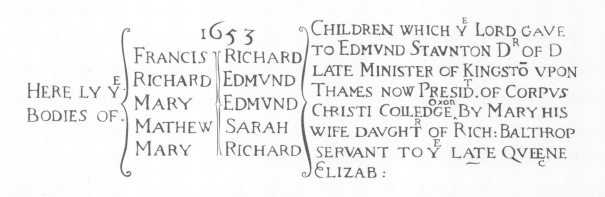

All Saints Church History
Victorian Times to the Present Day

Original Norman west door prior to
its demolition in the 1860s.

Church interior, 1883.

The eighteenth century, following the religious upheavals of the previous two centuries, which had led to Civil War, was marked by a serious but more restrained approach and a suspicion of 'enthusiasm' but at the end of the century the Church of England underwent an Evangelical Revival and the return of a more emotional approach to preaching. Samuel Gandy, vicar of Kingston from 1817 to 1851, was both an ardent Evangelical whose sermons were published after his death and also a clergyman who recognised that the growing population of the parish required the building of new churches. In the 1830s churches were built in outlying parts of the parish at Ham, Kingston Vale and Hook, and then in 1842 one was built in the suburb of Norbiton, about a mile from All Saints.

The Evangelical Revival was followed by the Oxford Movement which stimulated interest in the inheritance of the Church from early and medieval times. Gandy's successor, Henry Paul Measor, was concerned to improve the aesthetic standard of worship. This was not universally popular, and the *Surrey Comet* in 1857 lamented the influence that 'popery' was having on worship in All Saints. In 1867 Measor was succeeded by the Evangelical Alfred Williams, and Measor's changes in worship were reversed. The *Surrey Comet* lamented that services had been reduced to the "flat level of an old-fashioned village church".

In 1857-8 church rates were abolished in Kingston and replaced by voluntary subscription, ten years before these were abolished nationally by Act of Parliament. Towards the end of the century All Saints became more involved in education and charity. All Saints School was founded by the church in 1874. The Vicar, Winthrop Young, invited parishioners to show support for the school at prize-givings and other activities. By the end of 1878 the parish also had many social and charitable societies including a Sick and Poor Fund, a Parochial Library, a Bedding and Clothes Club, a Coal Club and a Bible Woman's Fund. Young also reversed Williams's changes, bringing All Saints into line with national developments in music and ceremonial.

All Saints, 1883.

All Saints was heavily restored by the Victorians. The first major phase, under the architect Raphael Brandon, took place in the 1860s. His work included removing the west gallery and the creation of the great west window with stained glass by Lavers and Barraud. The ceilings were also reconstructed. The original Norman west door was uncovered during restorations, but unfortunately it was judged incapable of being preserved, and it was photographed and destroyed.

The second phase of restoration was undertaken by John Loughborough Pearson in the 1880s. Pearson enlarged the two transepts, removed the remaining galleries and gave new roofs to the nave, aisles and transepts. The height of the east and west arches under the tower was raised. Most of our current stained glass dates from the second half of the nineteenth century.

After the First World War the Holy Trinity Chapel was refitted as the East Surrey Regiment Memorial Chapel. A choir vestry was built on the north side of the nave in 1925. These were the last substantial changes in the church until in 1978-9 the church was reordered by the architect Hugh Cawdron. The High Altar was placed beneath the tower with new choir stalls in the eastern bay of the nave. The Victorian pews were replaced by chairs. These changes reflected new approaches to worship and also the need for flexibility when the church was used for concerts and other events.

The interior of the church as we now see it is largely the result of a further reordering, combined with redecoration, by Ptolemy Dean in 2013-4. A new entrance was created on the north side of the church, opening All Saints up to the main commercial centre of the town. The altar was moved into a more or less central position in the nave, and the east end meets community needs.

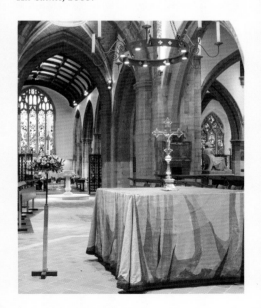

Church interior, 2015.

St Mary's Chapel

Medieval floor tile found on the site of St Mary's Chapel.

St Mary's was built in the eleventh century, probably before or shortly after the conquest of 1066.

When All Saints was built or rebuilt in the twelfth century, St Mary's stood to the south side of the church. The south transept of All Saints was later extended to join the north wall of St Mary's, which became its Lady Chapel.

By the late seventeenth century visitors noted that inside there were paintings of the Saxon kings rumoured to have been consecrated here, with captions stating that three of the kings were crowned here. Shortly after, the chapel was being used as a timber store for All Saints. The building collapsed in 1730, its foundations undermined by grave digging.

When the building collapsed, the sexton, Abram Hammerton, his son and his daughter Hester were trapped in the rubble. Abram died in the accident, but Hester and her brother were pulled from the rubble alive after seven hours. Hester had helped her father dig graves since she was 13 years old. She took over as sexton and became a well-known figure locally.

The site of St Mary's was excavated by William Finny, antiquary and mayor of Kingston, in 1926. It was found to have been 60 feet by 25 feet (roughly 18 metres by 7.5 metres) and have flint foundations. Floor tiles were discovered dating from the middle of the eleventh century and from the thirteenth century. Finny believed that St Mary's was built next to the ruins of an old Saxon church on All Saints' site, perhaps destroyed by Viking raids in the eleventh century.

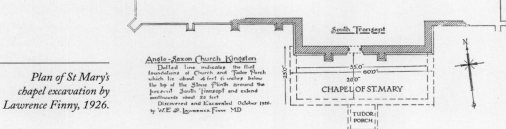

Plan of St Mary's chapel excavation by Lawrence Finny, 1926.

Only known surviving images of St Mary's Chapel, sketched before the building's collapse in the early eighteenth century and published in Manning and Bray's history of Surrey.

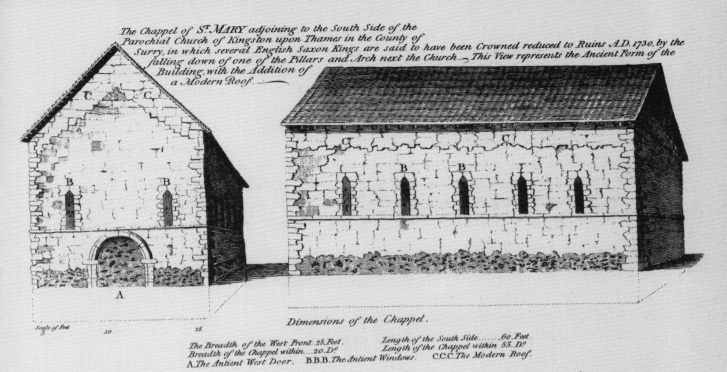

The Chappel of S.t MARY adjoining to the South Side of the
Parochial Church of Kingston upon Thames in the County of
Surry, in which several English Saxon Kings are said to have been Crowned reduced to Ruins A.D. 1730, by the
falling down of one of the Pillars and Arch next the Church. This View represents the Ancient Form of the
Building, with the Addition of
a Modern Roof.

Scale of Feet
5   10   25

Dimensions of the Chappel.

The Breadth of the West Front. 25.Feet.   Length of the South Side....... 60.Feet.
Breadth of the Chappel within ....20.D.°   Length of the Chappel within. 55.D.°
A.The Antient West Door.   B.B.B.The Antient Windows.   C.C.C.The Modern Roof.

This View represents the Modern Form of the Building A.D. 1726 when a
Draught of it was taken.

D.a Modern Window at the West End.   F.a Modern Porch.   G.a Modern Window at the East end.
E.E.Antient Windows Stopped up.

J.Basire sc.

23

Stained Glass

All Saints may well have had stained glass in some of its windows in the Middle Ages, but none of this has survived. Some may have been deliberately destroyed in the sixteenth and seventeenth centuries, and other glass simply replaced with plain glass as it suffered damage or when the stonework of the windows needed repair.

Most of the glass now in the windows is Victorian. These windows are by several of the leading firms of the period and are outstanding examples of High Victorian Gothic Revival. The earliest is the east window in the south choir aisle (2), by Ward & Nixon and probably from 1852. The great east window (1) is of 1860 by the same firm, now Ward & Hughes, and it was followed by windows by William Wailes (3), and Lavers and Barraud (4, 5, 11, 13, 19 all designed by Nathaniel Westlake; 12 possibly designed by Milner Allen; 21-2 in the clerestory) of whom Nathaniel Lavers was a member of the congregation. The great west window (12) is a particularly fine example of rich colouring and the figures of the Apostles with obviously Victorian heads are probably portraits of local people. Apart from no. 11 these all date from the 1860s. The windows of the south transept and the south wall of the nave (6-9) date from the period of Pearson's restoration in the 1880s and are by Burlison & Grylls, who were also responsible for no. 10, in 1920. These have lighter colouring and were influenced by late fifteenth century Flemish and German glass. With one exception the other windows are all of the twentieth century: nos 17 and 18 in the Holy Trinity chapel by Christopher Webb and the heraldic window (14) by Lowndes & Drury. The sole exception (15) is the fifteenth and sixteenth century glass from the Thomas and Drake collection installed in 1956. The windows were given as memorials, mainly to local people but in some cases to members of the East Surrey Regiment.

Most of the windows illustrate Bible stories or depict saints, but the heraldic window reflects All Saints' history. The lower left shield shows the arms which medieval heralds attributed to Edward the Elder, son of Alfred the Great and traditionally regarded as the first king to have been crowned at Kingston. To its right are the arms of Merton priory, patrons of the church in the Middle Ages. The priory was dissolved in 1538 and the patronage passed through various families until King's College Cambridge purchased it in 1786. The two upper shields bear the arms of King's College and King Henry VI, its founder.

East window of the vicars burial ground.

Memorials

The memorials in the church witness to the lives of benefactors and philanthropists and other notable local residents.

Sir Anthony Benn – The monument to Sir Anthony Benn (1570-1618), Recorder of Kingston and London, shows Benn in his lawyer's robes. He and his wife, Jane Evelyn, lived in Norbiton Hall. Benn was Recorder of Kingston and later of London. These were senior judicial offices.

Cesar Picton – This modest memorial is dedicated to Cesar Picton who died in 1836. Cesar was six years old when he was brought from Senegal to Kingston as a servant to Sir John Philipps of Norbiton Place. Cesar was left £100 by Lady Philipps when she died, which enabled him to establish a coal merchant's business in Kingston. By the time of his death Cesar was a wealthy man, both because of his successful business and bequests in the wills of all three Philipps daughters.

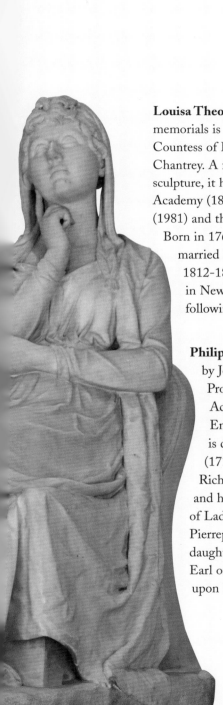

Louisa Theodosia – One of our most beautiful memorials is the statue of Louisa Theodosia, Countess of Liverpool, sculpted by Sir Francis Chantrey. A fine example of Chantrey's portrait sculpture, it has been exhibited at the Royal Academy (1824), the National Portrait Gallery (1981) and the Mappin Art Gallery (1981). Born in 1767, Louisa was 28 when she married Lord Liverpool, Prime Minister 1812-1827. They lived at Coombe House in New Malden, where Louisa died following a long illness in 1821.

Philip Medows – This monument is by John Flaxman who was the first Professor of Sculpture at the Royal Academy, and arguably the foremost English sculptor of the period. It is dedicated to Sir Philip Medows (1717-1781), deputy ranger of Richmond Park and husband of Lady Frances Pierrepont, daughter of the Earl of Kingston upon Hull.

Davidson family – This group memorial is dedicated to the Davidson family – Henry and Duncan Davidson, and Duncan's wife, son and daughter-in-law. The monuments are the work of Charles Regnart and John Ternouth, two distinguished sculptors. The Clan Davidson came from Tulloch in Scotland and were wealthy enough to own property in Scotland, Jamaica, South America and London. Although several members of the family were buried at All Saints no links to Kingston have yet been found.

John and Katherine Hertcombe – This badly damaged brass monument commemorates a Kingston merchant, John Hertcombe, and his wife Katherine. John, whose figure was stolen earlier last century, died on 22nd July 1488, Katherine having died earlier on 12th July 1477. She is shown wearing the elaborate headdress worn by fashionable ladies in the 15th century.

Memorial Chapel

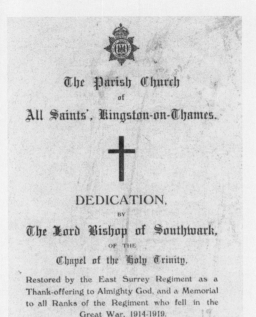

The Parish Church
of
All Saints', Kingston-on-Thames.

✝

DEDICATION,
BY
The Lord Bishop of Southwark,
OF THE
Chapel of the Holy Trinity,

Restored by the East Surrey Regiment as a
Thank-offering to Almighty God, and a Memorial
to all Ranks of the Regiment who fell in the
Great War, 1914-1919.

MAY 4th, 1921.

*Order of Service for the dedication
of the Memorial Chapel.*

The Chapel of Holy Trinity dates from the fifteenth century when the Fraternity of Holy Trinity was formed. In 1921 it was dedicated as the Regimental War Memorial of the East Surrey Regiment, who had long enjoyed close connections with Kingston.

The East Surrey Regiment's connection with Kingston dates back to 1782 when county titles were introduced for Regiments of Infantry. The 70th Regiment became the 70th Surrey Regiment and a Depot was established in Kingston to recruit local men. The barracks on Kings Road, Kingston were designed by the Royal Engineers and completed in 1875. In 1881 the 31st and 70th Regiments and the 3rd Battalion of the Royal Surrey Militia combined and became the East Surrey Regiment with the new barracks as their Depot. Around 84,000 men passed through the Depot and were trained there between 1914 and 1917 alone.

Work on restoring the Chapel of Holy Trinity was undertaken by friends and family of the Regiment in 1920, in memory of those who lost their lives in the First World War. The Chapel was dedicated by the Bishop of Southwark in 1921. On Armistice Day 1924 the Memorial Gates at the approach to the church from the market place were dedicated by the Bishop of Kingston. The memorial was further dedicated to those who lost their lives in the Second World War.

The Second World War saw the close connections between the Regiment and Kingston further solidified when, in May 1944, the Borough Council conferred the Freedom of the Borough on the regiment.

The East Surrey Regiment ceased to exist in 1959 when it amalgamated with The Queen's Royal Regiment to form The Queen's Royal Surrey Regiment. Its Old Comrades Association also amalgamated to form The Queen's Royal Surrey Regimental Association. In 1966 the Queen's Surreys became the 1st Battalion The Queen's Regiment, and subsequently joined with the Royal Hampshire Regiment to form The Princess of Wales's Royal Regiment.

The Queen's Royal Surrey Regimental Association continues its links with the Memorial Chapel at All Saints. Over the years it has made grants for refurbishments and improvements, and the Association still attends the annual Remembrance Day service as well as civic occasions in the Borough.

Today the Chapel is used as a place for prayer and contemplation. It contains Books of Remembrance, or 'of Life', containing the names of those killed in twentieth century conflict. The first was made and bound by the Hon. Norah Hewitt in memory of her brother, Captain the Hon. A R Hewitt DSO, who lost his life at Ypres on 25th April 1915. It was enlarged to record the names of the 1,198 members of the Regiment who lost their lives in 1939-45. The names of those who have died since 1945 are recorded in an additional book on the south side of the Chapel.

There are various memorials around the chapel. The oak panels on the walls are memorials to officers who served in the East Surrey Regiment. There is a section on the north wall commemorating those who hold the Victoria Cross. The Sanctuary Lamp was presented in 1913 by Major and Mrs J L Congdon, and burns in perpetual remembrance of those who died in 1914-18.

There is also a memorial plaque to the memory of General the Rt Hon Sir Edward Lugard GCB, Colonel, The East Surrey Regiment 1881-1898, situated on the south wall of the church. He was a very distinguished officer, having been promoted a Brevet Major for his exemplary conduct in the Battle of Sobraon.

There are two memorial windows of stained glass in the north wall. One is dedicated to the memory of Major General Sir John Longley KCMG, CB, Colonel, The East Surrey Regiment 1920-39, and his son Charles Raynsford Longley. Charles was killed at the Battle of Jutland in 1916, and the window was dedicated forty years later in January 1956. The second window is dedicated to the memory of Col H H W Pearse DSO. The hassocks (kneelers) in the chapel are in the regimental colours of maroon, amber and black.

Books of Remembrance containing the names of those killed in twentieth century conflict.

Memorial Chapel facing east.

Music and Choir

All Saints has a strong musical tradition. As early as the fourteenth century the church was given permission to run 'song schools' teaching children to chant and read. These would have been run by the vicar and any schoolmasters he appointed. By the sixteenth century All Saints had a choir which walked in ceremonial processions and sang at special services.

There was an organ in the church by 1509 at the latest, almost certainly on the rood loft and used to accompany plainsong at the main Sunday mass. By 1527 there were apparently two organs in the church. The 'quyer' at this time probably consisted of priests who participated in chanting and plainsong, perhaps with simple harmonisation.

After the Reformation, from 1570, there is no reference to the organ in the churchwardens' accounts for more than 200 years. There is also no specific evidence of a choir from the 1580s. Music in All Saints was probably restricted to the congregational singing of metrical psalms, led by the parish clerk. By the eighteenth century these were probably supplemented by hymns, which were permitted to be sung before and after the service. The clock in the tower was fitted with a carillon which played the tunes 'Hanover' (O Worship the King) and 'Easter Hymn' (Jesus Christ is Risen Today).

A new organ was erected in the west gallery in 1793 by public subscription. The organist employed was Mary Varden, a local girl from a musical family notable for her young age of 13. She was employed as organist for 40 years until her death. Mary is also notable for her high salary – in 1805 it was £30, almost the highest in the region, including the City of London, as her appointment coincided with a renewed emphasis on the singing of psalms.

Nave looking west in the early nineteenth century with the organ over the west door.

31

Music and Choir

Church Angels

Organists continued to be appointed as necessary, with Louisa Varden (Mary's sister) succeeding her in 1833. They were generally selected by competition, and always local women, until Elizabeth Kensett (organist from 1849) was replaced. After Elizabeth, only men were appointed to the role of organist. This is part of a wider trend across England, fuelled by the growth of a profitable music 'profession'. Some said that larger, modern organs were too physically challenging for women to play.

There was a choir of children and adults by 1817 at the latest, and probably considerably earlier. A new organ by Willis was installed in 1867, although almost immediately a new vicar reduced the scope of the music and the choirmen decamped to Hampton Court chapel. In 1877 the musical tradition was restored. From 1893 to 1954 Percy Alderson and then his son Philip, who are commemorated in the south porch, were successive organists. In 1958 an organ by Comptons replaced the much-altered Willis organ.

Over the past half-century the range and quality of music has continued to develop, and in 1988 an organ by the distinguished Danish builder Erik Frobenius was installed, to meet the needs of worship and secure All Saints as Kingston's leading venue for concerts as well as other dramatic and artistic events.

The choir, which includes both boys and girls, is known nationally for the quality of its music making and sings an extensive repertoire. As well as contributing to the worship of the church, it makes broadcasts and recordings, has excellent connections with local schools and has regularly produced choral scholars at Oxford and Cambridge Universities.

Organ by the distinguished Danish builder Frobenius install in 1988.

Memorials

1. Font
2. Medieval floor tiles
3. Robert and Joanna Skerne
4. Edmund Staunton and children
5. John and Katherine Hertcombe
6. Alderman William Cleave
7. Maria Lady Sharpeigh
8. Richard Mayo
9. St Blaise
10. Disney Hatchment
11. Louisa Theodosia Countess of Liverpool
12. Sir Anthony Benn
13. Anthony Fane
14. Peter De La Rive
15. Davidson Family
16. George Savage
17. Cesar Picton
18. John Heyton
19. William Dunbar
20. George Bate
21. Saxon Cross Shaft
22. Philip Medows
23. Nicholas Hardinge
24. The Beyer Stone
25. Roots Children
26. Robert Bardsey, Clement Mylam & Robert Hammond

Stained Glass

1. Great east window
2. Chancel south aisle east window
3. Chancel south wall eastern window
4. Chancel south wall western window
5. Vicars' burial ground east window
6. South transept window
7. South transept west aisle window
8. South aisle eastern window
9. South aisle central window
10. South aisle western window
11. South aisle west wall window
12. Great west window
13. North aisle west wall window
14. North aisle western window
15. North aisle eastern window
16. North transept window
17. Holy Trinity Chapel north wall western window
18. Holy Trinity Chapel north wall eastern window
19. Holy Trinity Chapel east window
20. Chancel north wall window
21. North clerestory window
22. South clerestory window